D0116592

BETTER WEIGHT TRAINING

George Sullivan

With photographs by Ann Hagen Griffiths

DODD, MEAD & COMPANY · NEW YORK

Library of Congress Cataloging in Publication Data

Sullivan, George, date
    Better weight training for boys.

    1. Weight lifting—Juvenile literature.
I. Griffiths, Ann Hagen. II. Title.
GV546.S94 1983   796.4'1   82–19871
ISBN 0–396–08121–5

Many people contributed in the preparation of this book. Special thanks are due Ann Hagen Griffiths for her excellent photographs; coach Morris Weissbrot for reading the manuscript for technical accuracy; Harvey Newton, U.S. Weightlifting Federation; Norman J. Liss, Liss Public Relations; Lee McConaughy, Merrilee Newman Matamales, and Jose Matamales.

The author is also grateful to John Capper, Xavier High School, New York City, and to Xavier students James Walsh, Bruce McLane, and Joseph Sweeney who posed for the photographs that appear in the book.

CONTENTS

BUILDING MUSCLE POWER

Exercise can make surprising changes in the human body. A regular, well-planned weight-training program can enable the average boy to increase his weight by several pounds, add inches to the measurement of his chest and thighs, and actually *double* his strength—and all of this within a period of six months.

Weight training is different from weight lifting or competitive body building. Weight training is not going to make it possible for you to clean and jerk 250 pounds or develop 18-inch biceps; no one is ever going to mistake you for Arnold Schwarzenegger.

Weight training means using relatively light weights to shape, strengthen, and condition the body as a whole. You not only look better, you feel better. You improve your skill in sports, indeed, in performing any activity that requires muscular strength.

"Weight training can be an important part of a personal development program through body conditioning," says Dr. Robert B. Greifinger, Medical Director of the Westchester Community Health Plan in White Plains, New York. "It can help improve coordination, strength, and self-esteem. The enhancement of balance, leverage, and coordination can come with body toning and increased strength.

These together help a young man in improving his sense of himself, increasing self-assuredness, and building self-esteem."

To understand the principles upon which weight training is based, you should know something about the body's mechanics, about muscles, tendons, and ligaments, and how they work together.

A muscle is a bundle of cells and fibers, called tissue, that moves a particular bone of the body when it is tightened or loosened.

There are three major types of muscle tissue in the body. Each has a different structure. Each plays a different role.

What are called involuntary muscles are those that line the internal organs. They operate without any conscious control on our part. Breathing, swallowing, and digestion are controlled by involuntary muscles.

Cardiac muscle is the second type. There is only one cardiac muscle. It forms the wall of the heart.

Skeletal muscles, the third type, are the muscles that control physical movement. They are the ones with which this book is concerned. There are 656 skeletal muscles in the body.

When you begin your weight-training program, it's important to understand that you cannot think in terms of exercising an individual muscle, a muscle that is isolated from all the others. Muscles work in groups. Thus, the chapters of this book are concerned with the development of the various muscle groups: the arm muscles, shoulder and neck muscles, and so forth.

Tendons and ligaments are other structures that you should know about. Tendons are the cords or bands of tough white, fibrous tissue at the ends of muscles. They connect muscles to bones.

Often during strenuous exercise, when you get a pain or an ache, it may be a tendon transmitting the message that you're overdoing. That's one reason why it's important to begin your training session with stretching exercises. They help to prepare the tendons for a full range of movement.

Ligaments are bands of tissue, usually white and fibrous, that connect one bone to another. The tightness of a ligament plays an important role in determining the flexibility of the joint it serves. For instance, the tightness of the ligaments at the sides of the knee that connect the thighbone (the femur) with the shinbone (the tibia) determine the flexibility of the knee.

When taking part in a strenuous exercise, you have to be careful not to stretch any ligament too far. Permanent damage can result. The joint can

Shown here are some of the important muscles of the body. They are discussed on the pages that follow, in connection with weight training exercises to develop them.

10

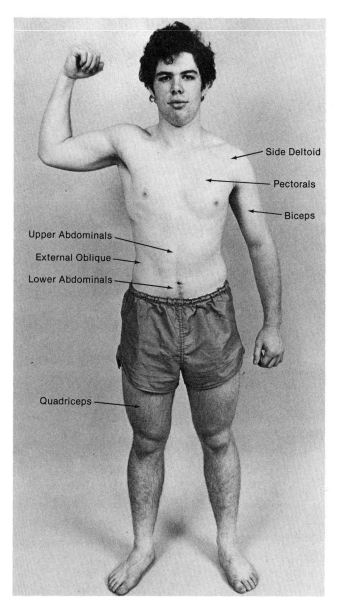

Side Deltoid

Pectorals

Biceps

Upper Abdominals

External Oblique

Lower Abdominals

Quadriceps

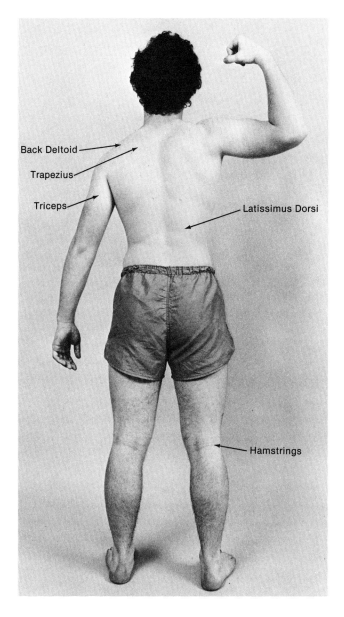

Back Deltoid

Trapezius

Triceps

Latissimus Dorsi

Hamstrings

become so "loose" that it will fail to perform properly. Such damage sometimes has to be repaired by surgery.

This is a reason why your exercise program has to be carefully paced. It's important to begin by lifting light weights, adding more weight very gradually.

Your body's nervous system plays a vital role in any weight-training program. The nervous system has two major divisions. There is the central nervous system which is made up of the brain and spinal cord. There is also the autonomic nervous system. This consists of the nerves and nerve tissue common to the blood vessels, heart, glands, and intestines, and which helps to control their functions.

When you perform some physical activity, such as bending over to pick a weighted object from the floor, all of these structures work together. The nerves stimulate muscles which move bones by means of the tendons near the joints which are held together by ligaments.

In weight training, what you do is apply an outside force to a specific muscle group. The muscle group tenses up, or contracts. Then when the outside force is removed, the muscles relax. Repeat this process on a regular basis and the muscle fibers begin to thicken, and the muscles themselves begin to increase in size.

What is actually happening is that the fibers are breaking down under the stress of lifting. They then

11

grow back stronger. In fact, they increase in size and strength in direct proportion to the amount of work you ask them to do.

The basic piece of equipment you use in "applying an outside force" is the barbell, a long steel bar with disc weights at each end. You also use dumbbells. A dumbbell has the same form as a barbell, except that its bar is less than a foot in length. The chapter that follows discusses barbells and dumbbells and other lifting equipment.

THE EQUIPMENT YOU NEED

Visit a modern gym or health club, and you're likely to be astonished by the great assortment of equipment available. There are strange-looking rollers and vibrating belts. There are rings and bars from which a person can chin or swing. There are big machines with weights attached to cables and pulleys.

But most of this is for advanced training programs. It takes only a few pieces of equipment to do the exercises described in this book.

The basic equipment you require consists of one long metal bar, from five to seven feet in length, two short bars, plus the weights—called plates—that attach to the bar ends. The plates weigh from 1½ pounds to 50 pounds apiece.

You also need the metal collars that hold the plates in place. Without collars, the plates would slip off the ends or slide toward the center.

The bar for the barbell should be fitted with a metal sleeve. When you grasp and lift, the sleeve revolves. Without the sleeve, the bar would tend to turn in your hand; you couldn't grip tightly.

If you visit a sporting goods store to buy your equipment, you may notice that some plates are made of metal and covered with plastic. Others are made of heavy-duty plastic and filled with sand or lead shot. While serious lifters often shun such plates, they are worthwhile because they're less likely to damage floors or furniture. You can thus

Metal collars like this one hold the plates in place.

exercise at home without being destructive.

Some weights are sold in one piece, that is, the plates are not removable. A five-pound dumbbell of this type always weighs five pounds. The failing of this type of equipment is that, as you become stronger, you can't add additional weight.

Bars and weights are usually sold in sets. A basic

13

These dumbbells have removable plates.

set for beginners is likely to include a barbell bar, two dumbbell bars, plus as many as ten plates that total as much as 160 pounds.

If you're planning on buying weights, look for a set in which the smallest plates weigh 1½ pounds. This allows you to add weight gradually, five pounds at a time. In some sets, the lightest plate weighs five pounds. Thus, when you want to add weight, you must add at least ten pounds, which is too much of a jump.

In addition to a barbell and pair of dumbbells, you should also have a padded weight bench. This enables you to do bench presses and a number of other exercises. When buying a bench, be sure it is sturdy enough to support not only your weight, but also the weight you intend to lift. It is not un-

common for such benches to be capable of supporting 1000 pounds.

Benches are often fitted with upright supports that hold a loaded barbell in place. You lie on your back on the bench and reach up to take the barbell from the rack. There are also squat racks that hold a loaded barbell at shoulder height while you get yourself into the correct lifting position.

Sporting goods stores sell weight-lifting "packages" that include everything you need—bars of barbell and dumbbell length, an assortment of plates, collars, a sleeve, a weight bench, and racks. A package usually costs between $100 and $150. Additional plates can be bought at anytime.

One of the good things about weight-training equipment is that it never wears out. You'll be able to use it the rest of your lifetime.

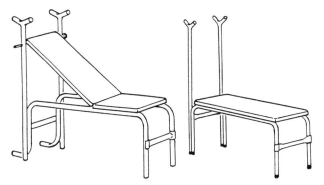

Two types of weight benches. Upright supports are for holding loaded barbells.

HOW TO EXERCISE WITH WEIGHTS

One advantage to weight training is that you can work out almost anywhere there is space for you and your equipment, plus a mirror in which you can check your form. You can work out at the school gym, at the local YMCA, or a health club. You can do your exercises in your living room or bedroom, the garage or basement.

As a beginner, the exercises you'll be doing will not be complicated. Unlike competitive weight lifting, where instruction and coaching are important, weight training doesn't require day-to-day supervision. This means that you're free to work out at home.

Be sure the room in which you do your exercises has good ventilation and is warm enough. The room temperature should be at least 65 degrees F. In a room that is cooler than that, you increase the risk of straining a muscle.

There are some disadvantages to working out at home. The fact that you're by yourself is one of them. When you train at the school gym, you'll be working out with other lifters. Some of them will be boys who have more lifting experience than you do. They'll give you tips that are sure to be helpful. Not only will you learn from them, but they'll be a source of inspiration. You'll get greater satisfaction out of your accomplishments. Overall, you're likely to try harder.

When you train by yourself, there is more of a tendency to skip a session when you're not feeling up to par, or just lazy. With a group, you feel more of a responsibility toward appearing at the gym on the designated days at the designated times. Another advantage of training at school is that you don't have to buy equipment.

The best situation of all is to be able to work out at school with your friends, but also to have lifting equipment at home. This makes it possible for you to work out on holidays, weekends, and during school vacation periods.

If it's not possible for you to work out at school, and you purchase weights and other equipment for home use, consider the possibility of teaming up with one or more of your friends. You'll then be able to enjoy some of the advantages of group training sessions.

Your workout should last from fifteen to thirty minutes. Less than fifteen minutes isn't likely to accomplish very much. More than thirty minutes can exhaust you, at least during the first weeks of your program. Once you become experienced, you can start increasing the amount of exercise time.

After a workout, your muscles should feel comfortably tired. You should never exercise to the point of exhaustion

Plan to exercise at least three or four times a week. If you decide on a three-day-a-week program, work out every other day—Monday, Wednesday, and Friday or Tuesday, Thursday, and Saturday. If you plan to work out four days a week, exercise the first day, skip a day, work out two days in a row, skip a day, work out, then skip a day—then start over again.

Exercising fewer than three times a week isn't likely to sufficently challenge you. On the other hand, a program in which you exercise five or more times a week is almost certain to tire your muscles, which need time to recover between workouts.

Try to do your exercises at the same time each day. Make them a habit. Some boys prefer working out in the morning, before leaving for school. Another good time is around three o'clock in the afternoon, after school. Or you can schedule your workouts later in the afternoon, an hour or so before dinner. After your workout, wait at least half an hour before you eat.

Always avoid exercising immediately after eating. Food needs at least half an hour to digest.

Some days you will feel stronger than others and your workouts will be a breeze. That's great. But don't add more weight to the barbell or increase the number of exercises you've planned. In other words, don't try to make too much progress too fast.

Other days you'll find your muscles tire quickly. On those days, take it a bit easier. No matter what, never force your body to do more than it seems capable of doing.

Toe touches are good for unlimbering.

There may be times when your program gets interrupted, perhaps because of an illness or a family vacation that takes you away from home.

16

In such cases, remember that you shouldn't restart your program at your previous level. It will take a few days to get your muscles back to the peak of condition you had achieved.

Once you start to experience results, your workouts are likely to cease being a chore. You'll begin to look forward to them. Indeed, exercising may get to be a hard habit to break.

Before you begin your workout, take time to stretch your muscles. The toe touch is one stretching exercise that you can perform. Stand with your feet comfortably apart and stretch your arms over your head, almost as if you were trying to touch the ceiling. Then, bending at the waist, sweep your right hand down and touch your left toe. Raise up again, pause, then touch your left hand to your right toe. Take it slowly. Don't force your muscles or tendons to stretch.

The sit-up is another good warm-up exercise. If you're not sure how to do a sit-up properly, read the description of it in the section of this book titled "Trimming Your Waist."

The hurdler's stretch is still another exercise that should be part of your warm-up routine. While in

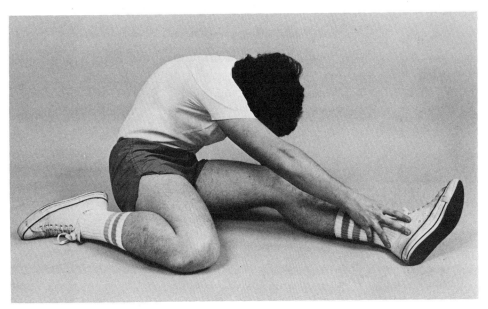

Hurdler's stretch is another standard warm-up drill.

17

a sitting position, bend your left leg to your side (so you're imitating the position of a hurdler as he goes over the bar). Keep the right leg straight. Leaning forward from the waist, reach with both hands to touch or grasp your outstretched ankle or foot. If you're really limber, you may be able to touch your toes. Hold the position for a count of ten.

Then lean back in the other direction. The left leg should still be folded back. Go back slowly; lean as far as you can. Reverse the position of your legs and do the exercise again.

Finish up your warm-up session with several jumping jacks or by jogging in place briefly.

When you train with weights, there are two variables involved: how much weight you lift, and how many times you lift it without stopping and resting, that is, the number of repetitions you do.

When you repeat one exercise eight times, say, without stopping and resting, you have performed one set of eight repetitions. Once eight repetitions no longer offer a real challenge, you add another repetition.

When you can increase the number of repetitions to twelve, and can perform twelve "reps" with relative ease, you then add more weight to the barbell, 2½ pounds at each end. Then begin the sequence of repetitions at eight again.

Another means of development involves doing additional sets. For instance, after performing eight repetitions—one set—you rest a minute or so, and then do another set. Then you rest again and do a third set.

How much weight should you, as a beginner, lift during a training session? That's a difficult question. The answer depends on your age, size, build, and other factors.

If you've never lifted weights before at all, spend time experimenting with the lifting equipment. The first time you try a bench press, remove all weight from the bar. In other words, press only the bar itself (which weighs about 25 pounds). Add weight in five pound steps (2½ pounds at each end of the bar) until you arrive at a point where the amount of weight you're pressing challenges you but is still not difficult to handle. That's your starting point.

One rule of thumb states that as a beginner you should select no more than one-half of your body's weight when doing presses, and no more than one-third of your weight when doing curls. (A curl is an exercise in which a barbell or dumbbell is raised from the thigh to shoulder level using only the muscles, chiefly of the biceps.)

Keep in mind that heavy lifting, that is, lifting an amount of weight that makes you really work, is what builds strength and increases muscle size. As an example, let's take the bench press, an exercise in which the lifter lies on his back and then, using the arms, shoulders, and chest, thrusts the barbell up from his chest. Suppose you have "pressed" 80 pounds eight times for three sets. If your goal is to increase muscle strength, you'd then be thinking in terms of increasing the weight to 85 or 90 pounds, and decreasing the number of reps to five or six. Once you had mastered that test, you'd increase the weight to 95 or 100 pounds and reduce the reps to three or four, and so on.

On the other hand, lighter lifting, that is, lifting less weight for a greater number of reps, improves muscle quality and tone, and also increases endurance. Once again, suppose you have been successful in pressing 80 pounds eight times for three sets. If your ambition is to improve the quality of your muscles, then you'd be thinking in terms of increasing the number of reps, not the amount of weight. You'd add a rep, pressing 80 pounds nine times for three sets. Once you could do that successfully, you'd add another rep, a tenth rep, and you'd continue to add them until you had reached twelve, thirteen, fourteen, or even twenty—whatever target you had established.

The sections of this book that follow, and which describe specific exercises for you to do, recommend gripping the barbell or dumbbells with either an overhand or underhand grip. In an overhand grip, the knuckles are placed above the bar. In an underhand grip, the knuckles are below the bar.

Sometimes it can be difficult to distinguish one type of grip from the other, as when, for example, you're holding a dumbbell in back of your shoulders

The underhand grip (above) and overhand grip.

or head. In such cases, simply bring the dumbbell to a position in front of your body—or imagine moving it there—and you'll realize immediately which type of grip is being used.

You should pay special attention to your grip. Don't take it for granted. When you have a strong grip, you get a quicker and more powerful response from the muscles of your upper body. A strong grip makes lifting easier.

Wrist curls and reverse curls are among the exercises that will help you develop a stronger grip. Repeatedly squeezing a rubber ball is another exercise that is recommended.

When lifting and performing the other drills described in this book, you should learn to control your breathing. Inhale as you prepare to lift; exhale as you strain.

One noted body-builder tells his pupils to think of inhaling as "stoking the furnace." It creates the strength that is needed during the period of exertion.

When doing a bench press, inhale as you lower the weight to your chest, exhale when you press it to arm's length. In the half squat, inhale as you lower yourself into the squat position, and exhale as you rise.

Concentrate on developing proper breathing rhythm from the start. Make it a natural part of your lifting routine.

Once you begin lifting on a regular basis, it's a good idea to keep a record of your progress. Make a chart with columns in which you record the date of your workout, the name of the exercise, the amount of weight involved, and the number of repetitions and sets you perform. After just a few sessions, the chart should begin to serve as evidence of the improvement you're making.

Weight training is one of the safest of all athletic activities. There's no other competitor involved, no other individual who is trying to outdo you. There is no "enemy" player. There is no built-in violence. But since weight training does put your muscles under greater-than-normal stress, there is a risk that you can suffer an injury.

Strains and sprains are the most common forms of injury. A strain is different from a sprain. A strain occurs when you overuse or overexert muscles or tendons. Strains usually aren't serious, but the pain associated with them can prevent you from working out for days or even weeks.

A sprain involves one or more ligaments and results when you overstrain or wrench an ankle or wrist or some other part of the body at a joint. The signs of a sprain are rapid swelling, skin discoloration (as if the area were bruised), and inability to use the joint.

To treat a minor sprain, place an ice cube on the surface of the skin, and move it about in a circular pattern for several minutes. This should reduce the pain and prevent additional swelling.

Have the injury examined by a physician. He or she is likely to recommend X-rays to rule out the possibility of a fracture.

Weight lifters also experience muscle cramps from time to time. A cramp occurs when a muscle suddenly contracts—shortens—then stays contracted. Light massage usually provides relief. The application of heat can also be helpful.

If you experience cramps frequently, there may be something wrong with your diet. Too much protein and not enough calcium could be the cause of the problem.

More serious injuries include torn muscles or ligaments, neck sprains, and hernias. A hernia is a split or tear in a fibous muscle sheath, something like the rip that might occur in a tight pair of jeans when the wearer bends over.

When the muscle sheath tears, the contents spill out. A hernia requires medical attention.

Injuries usually result from carelessness or mistakes. By following these precautions, you can help prevent injury:

• Work with an amount of weight that is appropriate for your size, build, and experience. Don't hesitate about getting advice on this subject from

Each plate is stamped with its weight. Be sure to double-check that both sides of the barbell are loaded with plates of exactly the same weight.

21

a coach or trainer. Working with too much weight is a frequent cause of injury.

• Always warm up thoroughly. Spend at least ten minutes unlimbering.

• Always use the correct lifting technique. Injuries sometimes occur because the victim fails to control or balance the weight properly, and too much strain results. This can be true even in the case of light weights. Never allow yourself to become careless when it comes to technique. Have a full-length mirror available so that you can check your form.

• Be sure the weights are properly balanced. Double-check to see that one side of the barbell is not heavier than the other. Even a few pounds of extra weight at one end can cause a painful muscle cramp.

• Don't lift when your muscles are tired. Strains frequently occur on the lift's final set.

• Make progress gradually. Don't be so eager to excel that you try to do too many exercises too soon. Success in weight training is achieved on a step-by-step basis.

A final word: Always pay attention to what you're doing. Concentrate on the exercise and the way in which you're performing it. By concentrating you reduce the chances of making a mistake.

ARM EXERCISES

Every individual who embarks upon a weight-training program wants to develop muscular arms. Big biceps are as popular a goal as a flat belly. But the biceps, which is the muscle at the front of the upper arm, is not as important as the triceps. The triceps, much larger than the biceps, forms the back of the upper arm. In all lifts in which weights are raised overhead from the floor, the biceps plays only a secondary role. The triceps (plus the leg and back muscles) do the bulk of the work.

TRICEPS EXTENSION—This exercise is performed with a single lightweight dumbbell. Grasp it in your right hand, using an overhand grip. Clamp the left hand over the right.

Hold the dumbbell directly above your head, then, bending your arms at the elbows, lower it directly behind your neck: pause, then raise the dumbbell up over your head again.

Remember, it's only your hands and forearms that move, your elbows acting as a hinge.

This exercise both stretches and contracts the triceps. Even when performed with a lightweight dumbbell, it is likely to cause some muscle soreness the first time you do it with any frequency. You can work out the soreness by doing the exercise with a dumbbell of lighter weight.

Other exercises important in developing the triceps are included in the section of this book titled

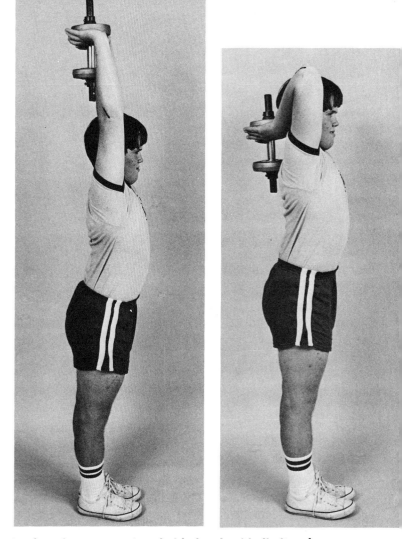

In the triceps extension, hold the dumbbell directly above your head, then lower it behind your neck.

23

Barbell curls help develop the biceps. Use an underhand grip, raising the bar from thigh to shoulder level, your elbows acting as a hinge.

"Shoulder and Neck Exercises," which follows.

BARBELL CURL—The barbell curl is the standard exercise to use in strengthening the biceps, the muscle at the front of the upper arm.

Grasp the barbell with an underhand grip, keeping your hands comfortably apart. Stand with your arms hanging straight down. Rest the barbell on your thighs.

Raise the barbell—curl it—to your chin. Keep your elbows close to your sides as you bring the bar up. Then lower the bar smoothly to the starting position.

Don't get the muscles of your back involved. This is an exercise chiefly for the biceps. You should feel them doing the work.

Do six to eight repetitions and work up to three sets. Then try to increase the number of repetitions in each set. When you can do twelve repetitions easily, try increasing the barbell weight by five pounds.

REVERSE CURL—This exercise is the same as the one described above, except that you use an over-

For reverse curls, use an overhand grip. This exercise helps strengthen forearm muscles.

Curling with dumbbells is good for the biceps. The dumbbells should touch the shoulders at the finish.

hand grip. When you do reverse curls, you make the forearm muscles work harder. The biceps, however, work less. This means that you won't be able to use as much weight for your reverse curls as you did for the standard curls.

DUMBBELL CURL—You can also perform curls

with dumbbells. One advantage of using dumbbells is that they require you to do an equal amount of work with each arm. When you perform a curl using a barbell, there is always the chance that a greater amount of work will be done by the stronger arm.

Stand erect holding a dumbbell in each hand, allowing them to hang at your sides. Use an underhand grip.

Slowly raise the dumbbell toward your shoulders. Turn your hands as you lift so the thumbs point outward. When the dumbbells touch your shoulders, pause, then lower them to the starting position.

Naturally, there's no need to perform barbell curls and dumbbell curls in the same workout.

Choose the type of equipment that appeals to you the most.

WRIST CURL—This exercise focuses upon the forearms. It's done from a seated position, with only the hands and wrists moving.

As you sit, hold a barbell with an underhand grip. Rest your forearms on your thighs and upper legs. Then raise the barbell by moving only your hands and wrists. Pause, then lower it to the starting position.

You can also do this exercise as a reverse curl, that is, while using an overhand grip. And, of course, it can be performed with dumbbells as well as with a barbell.

When you do wrist curls, only your hands and wrists move.

SHOULDER AND NECK EXERCISES

The muscles of the shoulders and neck are important to a great many athletic activities. They're the muscles that put distance into baseball throws and power into tennis strokes. In basketball, football, and swimming, they're in constant use. They're

28

In doing the overhead press, reach for the dumbbell, bending at the waist and knees. Raise the bar to shoulder level, then push it overhead.

vital to such field events as the javelin, shot put, discus, and pole vault. And it is these muscles that enable you to lift weights to levels above your head.

The deltoid and the trapezius muscles are the most important of the shoulder muscles. The deltoid, a large triangular muscle, caps the shoulder almost like a pair of football shoulder pads. The trapezius, also of good size, is a flat muscle that forms much of the upper and back part of the shoulders and the neck. A well-formed trapezius helps in maintaining good posture.

THE OVERHEAD PRESS—While it is one of the basic exercises of virtually every weight-training program, the overhead press is one that you should approach with some caution. Don't be afraid to start with the bar lightly weighted. Some coaches, in fact, have young lifters begin with an empty bar. Once the lifter gets the "feel" of pressing, a small amount of weight is added. The deltoid and triceps muscles are both strengthened by the overhead press.

Be sure you are well balanced to prevent straining your lower back. This means that you should bend your knees slightly as you lift. Be sure your feet are comfortably apart. Use an overhand grip, your hands a bit wider than shoulder-width apart.

Begin with the barbell on the floor in front of you. Bending at the waist and knees, reach down to take a firm grip.

This is upright rowing. From thigh level, simply pull the bar to your chin.

Straighten up and swing the barbell to shoulder level. Tuck your elbows to your side. Hold the bar firmly against the front of your shoulders and the collarbone.

Next, push the bar past your face to a point over your head. Keep pushing until your arms are fully extended. (In the vocabulary of weight lifting, you've just "pressed" the bar.) Pause for a moment at the top. Then slowly lower the bar to the starting position at the shoulders.

Press the bar up again, pause at the top, then return the bar to shoulder level. Press up again and return. If you don't tire, try as many as six or eight repetitions.

You can also perform this exercise with a pair of dumbbells. Hold them just outside your shoulders at the start, so the plates are close to or perhaps even touching the outside of your shoulders. Then press them upward until your arms are fully extended.

UPRIGHT ROWING—This is another basic drill for building the shoulder muscles, particularly the trapezius muscle. It also helps in shaping and forming the biceps.

With the bar on the floor in front of you, reach down and grasp it with an overhand grip. This time, however, your hands should be spaced only about six inches apart. Your feet should be comfortably apart.

Straighten up and let your arms hang straight, the barbell resting across your thighs.

Keeping your hands close to your body, and without shifting them on the bar, pull the bar to a point just below the level of your chin. Keep your elbows higher than the bar. Pause for a moment at the top, then lower the bar until your arms are fully extended again and the bar is at the starting position. Repeat the exercise six or eight times.

This is not an easy exercise. You may want to try less weight than the amount you used in the overhead press. Some lifters, in an effort to make the drill easier, start swinging the bar up and out, instead of lifting it straight up. Swinging the bar does make the drill easier, of course, but it sharply reduces the value of the exercise. Cheaters never win.

LATERAL RAISE—This is an easy-to-do exercise that is good for the deltoid muscle. Stand with a dumbbell in each hand, using an overhand grip, letting the weights hang at your sides.

Then, keeping your arms almost straight, raise the dumbbells until they are above the level of your head. Pause for a moment, then lower the weights to the starting position, and repeat.

As you do this exercise, resist the tendency of turning your wrists so that your thumbs begin to point toward the ceiling. In fact, do the opposite; tilt the weights so the front ends point downward slightly.

A variation of this exercise is to lift while bending. Lean well forward from the waist. Your back should be about parallel with the floor. You have a dumbbell in each hand, holding them with an overhand grip.

The lateral raise strengthens the deltoids. Hold a dumbbell in each hand. Keeping your arms almost straight, raise the dumbbells until they're just above shoulder level.

Let your arms hang straight down. While still leaning forward and keeping your arms straight, raise the dumbbells to the level of your chest. Pause, then lower the weights to the starting position.

SHOULDER SHRUG—At first glance, this drill may appear quite trivial, yet it has important value in developing the trapezius muscle. Don't neglect it.

Standing erect, hold a dumbbell in each hand at arm's length. Then raise your shoulders upward, as if you were shrugging. Try to touch your ears with the tops of your shoulders. Before you lower the shoulders to the starting position, pull them back as far as you can.

Repeat the exercise at least eight to ten times.

The exercises described in the paragraphs that follow help to strengthen the muscles of your neck. If possible, they should be done on a mat or rug. Also place a folded towel under your head for cushioning.

NECK BRIDGE—Lie flat on your back with your knees well bent and the soles of your feet flat to the floor or mat. Slide your feet close to your buttocks and fold your arms across your chest. Pushing from your soles and the top of your head, raise your thighs, buttocks, and shoulders from the mat, forming an arch with your body. Pause, then let your

Shoulder shrugs are good for the trapezius muscle. Try to touch your shoulders to your ear lobes.

33

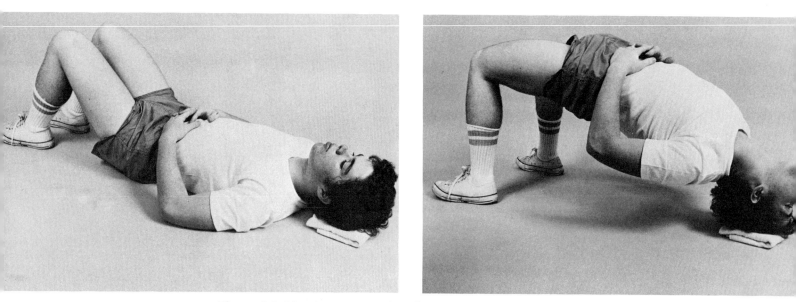

The neck bridge is not easy. The idea is to form an arch with your body. Your soles and the top of your head are your support points.

body down slowly. Repeat the exercise. Strive to do five or ten repetitions.

NECK BRIDGE WITH DUMBBELL—Don't try this exercise until your neck muscles are very strong, and then attempt it only with a lightweight dumbbell.

Again, lie flat on your back and pull your feet close to your buttocks. Place the dumbbell behind your head and grip it firmly with both hands, one overlapping the other. Bring the dumbbell to your chest and then press it straight up. Then, pushing from the soles and the back of your head, arch your body, forming a bridge. Pause, lower your body, then lower the dumbbell to your chest. Then repeat the exercise.

This is not an easy drill. Indeed, some athletes never master it. Be certain that you can perform the standard neck bridge—without any dumbbell— before you try it.

Be sure you can do the standard neck bridge before you attempt the exercise with a dumbbell. Press the dumbbell straight up, then form a bridge with your body.

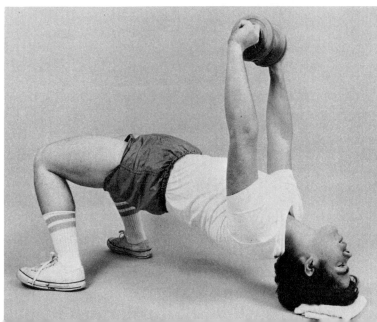

BACK EXERCISES

The latissimus dorsi is a broad flat muscle on each side of the back, running from under the arms to the waist. When a weight lifter says that he is working on developing his "lats," the latissimus dorsi is what he's talking about. When well-developed, this muscle serves to taper the back, giving it a V-shape, something every lifter strives for.

CHIN-UP—One of the best exercises for strengthening the latissimus dorsi is that old standby, the chin-up. While you're not likely to have a chinning bar at home, perhaps there is one available in your school gym.

Practice the chin-up with either an overhand or underhand grip, whichever feels the best. Grasp the bar with your hands positioned about shoulder-width apart. Begin the exercise with your arms fully extended, take a deep breath, and raise your body until your chin is above bar level. Return to the starting position, and exhale.

Try to do the exercise ten times. If you can't, do as many as you can each time you work out, and try adding one to your total each week.

If you're able to perform chin-ups with ease, try doing as many as three sets of ten. If that gets to be easy for you, add some weight. Use a length of rope or a belt to tie a 2½- or five-pound barbell plate to your waist. Adding weight, however, is not something a beginner should try.

36

Chin-up, performed here with an underhand grip, is standard exercise for strengthening the latissimus dorsi muscle, found on each side of the lower back.

BENT-OVER ROWING—This is an exercise that is somewhat the same as the upright rowing drill, explained in the section of this book devoted to "Shoulder and Neck Exercises." Your hands and arms move in somewhat the same fashion as they do when rowing a boat. Not only does the exercise help to broaden the back, but it contributes generally to upper body strength.

Stand with the barbell on the floor in front of you. Be sure your feet are comfortably apart. Bending from the waist and knees, reach down and grasp the bar with an overhand grip. Keep your hands slightly more than shoulder-width apart.

Lift the weight just off the floor. Keep your upper body parallel to the floor as you do so. Let the bar hang at arm's length. Your knees should be slightly bent.

Maintaining your bent-over position, lift the bar until it touches your chest. Pause for a moment, then slowly lower the bar until your arms are fully extended again.

This is another exercise that can cause a strained back, if you're not careful. Be certain the amount of weight you seek to lift tends toward the light side. And also be certain to keep your knees slightly bent —never let them lock—as you lift. With bent knees,

In bent-over rowing, begin with the barbell in front of you. Lift it off the floor, letting it hang at arm's length, then raise it to chest level.

you're able to keep fully balanced and at the same time you cause your legs to do at least part of the lifting.

Bent-over Lateral Raise—The arm action in this exercise is similar to that of the flyaway, described in the chapter that follows. But instead of lying on your back, you are standing and bent at the waist.

Grasp a dumbbell in each hand, using an overhand grip. Bend over until your upper body is

The bent-over lateral raise is executed with the upper body parallel to the floor. Raise the dumbbells to shoulder level, then return them to the starting position.

parallel to the floor. Be sure your feet are comfortably apart. Bend your knees slightly. Let the weights hang down in front of you. Then raise them smoothly to shoulder level, keeping your arms straight as you do so. Return the weights slowly to the starting position, and repeat. Besides strengthening the back, this exercise develops the shoulder muscles.

THE DEAD LIFT—The dead lift permits you to lift a tremendous amount of weight. But make progress slowly. When done in the manner described here, the exercise strengthens the muscles of the lower back plus the thighs and hips.

With the barbell on the floor in front of you, place your feet comfortably apart and, bending in the knees, reach down and grasp the bar, keeping your hands about shoulder-width apart. Some individuals use an overhand grip, but others find it easier to lift having one hand grip with an overhand grip, the other with an underhand grip (as shown).

Keep your chin up, your back straight.

To lift, simply straighen up. Pause, the barbell resting across your thighs. Then lower the bar to the starting position and repeat.

The dead lift involves reaching down to grasp a well-weighted bar, straightening up, then holding the bar at thigh level.

Push-ups are highly regarded for developing the chest, biceps, and shoulders. Begin with your body raised so a straight line is formed from the back of your head to the back of your heels. Then lower your body until your chest just touches the floor.

CHEST EXERCISES

Chest exercises are perhaps the most rewarding of all, for they produce quite noticeable results, giving a strong, rugged look to the upper body.

Technically speaking, it is the pectoral muscles—"pecs," as weight lifters call them—that are most strengthened and developed by the exercises offered in this section. The pectorals are fairly large muscles that cover the entire chest. These exercises also help to develop the muscles of the shoulders and arms and, to some extent, the latissimus dorsi—the "lats"—that give breadth to the back.

PUSH-UP—Just because you've known this exercise since your grade-school days, don't ignore it. It's hard to beat for developing the chest, biceps, and shoulders.

Lie face down on the floor, your palms about shoulder-width apart, your fingers pointing straight ahead. Push yourself up off the floor, straightening your arms. Your body should be in a straight line from the back of your head to the back of your feet. This is your starting position.

Taking a deep breath, lower your body until your chest just brushes the floor. Then raise yourself to the starting position, and exhale. Begin with

41

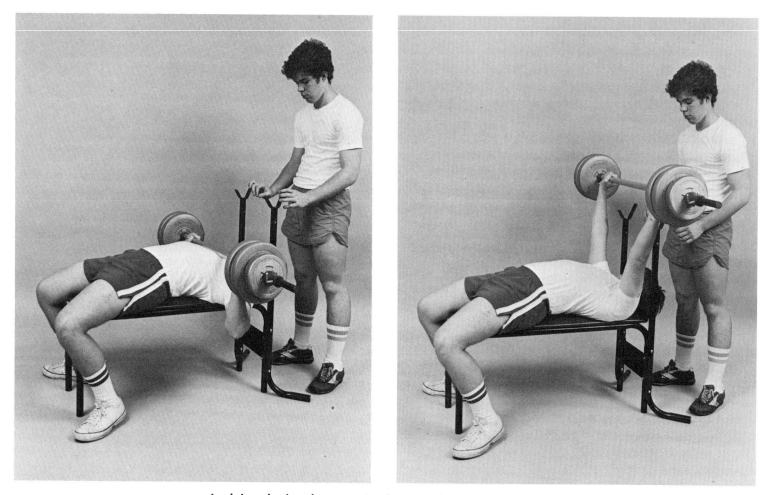

In doing the bench press, simply press the bar above your
chest, straightening your arms. A spotter should assist you.

five or ten repetitions, working up to fifteen.

After you've completed a few months of weight training, and are capable of doing as many as thirty push-ups without great difficulty, try some push-up variations. You can, for example, try doing push-ups on your fingertips. Or try this: stand between the backs of two chairs, grasping the top of each. Then raise your body until your arms are fully extended, tucking your feet up under your torso. Then, taking a deep breath, lower yourself as far as you can go. Then return to the starting position and dip down again. There's no chance you'll do *this* thirty times!

Still another variation is to first assume the push-up starting position, your arms straight, your body straight. Then have someone place a five- or ten-pound barbell plate on your upper back. Then do your push-ups.

BENCH PRESS—This is one of the best of the upper-body exercises, good for the pectoral muscles, the biceps, and the shoulders.

Lie on your back on a bench, your legs extending over the bench end, your feet flat to the floor. Hold the barbell across your chest, grasping it with an overhand grip. Position your hands slightly wider than shoulder-width apart.

Press the bar above your chest, straightening your arms. Pause, then lower the weight smoothly until the bar just touches the lower part of your chest, then immediately press it back up.

Always exhale as you press the bar up; inhale as you lower it.

This exercise can also be done from the floor, of course. But the bench is better because it enables you to lower the bar all the way to your chest, and this is necessary to fully exercise the pectoral muscles.

Very heavy weights can be lifted in the bench press, once your muscles have been strengthened. For example, high school football coaches expect each player to be able to press an amount of weight that is at least equal to his own. And it is by no means exceptional for a high school athlete to press fifty pounds more than his weight.

Once you begin to press heavy weights, it's a good idea to have a friend serve as a spotter. He can assist you in getting the bar into position at the start and come to your aid should you begin to tire with the bar in an elevated position.

FLYAWAY—This exercise gets its name because the arm action involved resembles the beating of a bird's wing in flight. It's called the "fly" for short. If you're technically minded, you can refer to it as a bent-arm lateral raise.

You can do the exercise while on the floor or bench. It's a bit more effective when done on the bench, however.

Lie on your back, your arms out to the sides, a dumbbell in each hand. Use an underhand grip.

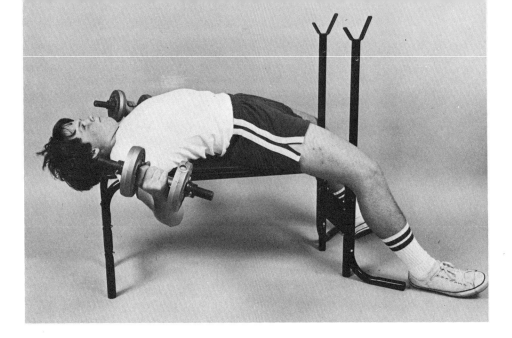

Lie on your back to do the fly-away. Raise the dumbbells until you can touch them together, then lower them slowly to the starting position.

Begin the straight-arm pullover by first pressing the barbell over your chest . . .

Bending your elbows slightly, slowly raise the dumbbells until you can lightly touch them above your head. Then slowly lower them to the starting position. Inhale as you're lowering the weights to your sides. Exhale as you raise them.

STRAIGHT-ARM PULLOVER—This is an exercise that strengthens the muscles of the chest and upper back, and also stretches and enlarges the rib cage. You can use a single dumbbell to do the exercise, holding it with both hands, or you can use a bar-

bell, grasping it with the hands shoulder-width apart. The barbell is best.

Lying on a bench, press the barbell directly over your chest. Then slowly lower the weight backward, keeping your arms straight. Lower it behind your head as far as you can without straining yourself. When you've reached that point, pause, then slowly raise the weight to the starting position.

Time your breathing with the raising and lowering of the weight. As you lower it, inhale steadily so

45

. . . then slowly lower it backward until it touches the floor.

that your lungs are filled just as the barbell reaches the lowest point. Exhale as you raise it.

When you can do the straight-arm pullover easily, there is a variation you can try. Move forward on the bench so that your head hangs over the end. Place the barbell on the floor in back of you. Using an overhand grip, your hands only six to eight inches apart, and with your arms well bent, raise the barbell up over your face, allowing it to come to rest—briefly—on your chest. Then lower the weight to the starting position and repeat the exercise.

This is called the bent-arm pullover. It's good for developing the chest and upper back. But, remember, it's not for beginners.

46

In doing the half squat, begin from an erect position. Squat down until the undersides of your thighs are parallel to the floor.

LEG AND THIGH EXERCISES

The muscles of the legs and thighs are the body's largest and most powerful. Not only are they important on account of their size, but also because virtually every human activity requires leg and thigh power.

THE HALF SQUAT—While this exercise is especially good for the thighs, it also helps in conditioning the muscles of the belly, the lower back, and the buttocks.

Be sure you realize that it is a *half* squat. You lower your body only part of the way.

One problem with this exercise is that you can't

47

do it alone, unless you have a stand on which to place the barbell as you get it into position. If you don't have a stand, you need two spotters to help you.

Begin the exercise from an erect position, the bar centered upon your upper back and shoulder just below the back of your neck. (If this feels uncomfortable, place a folded towel under the bar as padding.) Use an overhand grip, placing the hands well apart on the bar. Place your feet comfortably apart, your toes pointing slightly outward.

Squat slowly, bending at the knees until the undersides of your thighs are about parallel to the floor. Keep your chin up. Don't arch your back.

Once your thighs are parallel to the floor, rise up to the starting position. As you do, concentrate on pushing with your legs, not lifting with your back.

There is a special way to breathe when performing the half squat. You should always inhale when going down, and exhale when coming up.

If you find it hard to judge when you are low enough in the squat, place a bench or a chair behind you. Adjust the level of the bench so that when you reach the half-squat position, you just touch it with your buttocks. This signals that you're low enough and should start to raise up.

If done faithfully, this exercise can enable you to build great strength. But in the early stages, be cautious about the amount of weight you use. And never, even when you become experienced, attempt to do the exercise without spotters to assist you.

FRONT SQUAT—This, too, is a half squat, but with the bar held in front of the body, across the upper chest and shoulders. Since you're not able to get as much leverage as in the half squat (described above), you're not able to handle as much weight.

But a benefit of the front squat is that you don't need anyone's assistance in lifting the bar into the starting position. You're thus able to do this exercise at home by yourself. Another plus is that the front squat reduces the tendency to bend your back as you lift, making the chances of back injury less likely.

With your feet about shoulder-width apart, the toes pointed slightly outward, bend down and grasp the bar with an overhand grip. Your hands should be wide apart on the bar, well outside the shoulders, in fact. Lift the bar to shoulder level, letting it come to rest across your upper chest. (Since getting the weight into position is not part of the actual exercise, you can use other muscles to help "swing" the bar up.) Once the bar is in place, your elbows should be pointing straight forward as you grip the bar.

Begin from a standing position. Bend at the knees, lowering your upper body until you reach a half-squat position, that is, until your thighs are just about parallel to the floor. (Use a chair or bench to signal when you've reached a half squat,

The front squat is a half squat, too. When the undersides of your thighs become parallel to the floor, rise to a standing position again.

as described above.) Keep your chin up; keep your back straight.

Once your thighs are about parallel to the floor, rise immediately. Remember to inhale as you're going down, to exhale when rising up.

LUNGES—This exercise is helpful in developing

49

the muscles at the front of the thighs (the quadriceps) and also those at the back of the thighbone and the knee (the hamstring). You need assistance to do the exercise because it involves placing the barbell across the upper back and shoulders, as in the half squat (see above).

Once the bar is in place, stand erect. Keep your back straight and your chin up. Your feet should be about shoulder-width apart.

Take a full step forward with your left foot, and then bend the left knee so that the left thigh comes parallel to the floor. The right knee should bend too, of course.

From this position, push yourself back, returning to the starting position. Now repeat the exercise, stepping with the other foot. Keep alternating until you've done at least eight repetitions with each leg.

It's important to remember to keep your back straight. If you allow yourself to bend forward at the hips, you'll put too much strain on your lower back. Instead, you must keep the weight centered over your hips.

The first few times you try this exercise, do it in front of a mirror. This will help you in keeping your upper body properly balanced.

In performing lunges, place the barbell across your upper back and shoulders, then stride forward, bending the striding leg and rear leg as shown.

CALF RAISES—The calf is the fleshy part of the leg just below the back of the knee. Strong calves are necessary for quick movement. Sprinters need strong calves to be able to explode out of the blocks. They're also important in such sports as basketball, tennis, and football.

Calf raises, which are meant to strengthen the calves, can be done while seated or standing. In addition to a properly weighted barbell, you need a short length of board that is about two inches thick, or a book or some other similarly shaped object of that thickness. The board is placed beneath the toes in performing the exercise.

When doing seated calf raises, sit on a bench or chair with the barbell resting across your knees. (You can place a folded towel across your knees as padding.) Hold the bar in place with an overhand grip.

As you sit, raise the balls of your feet, lifting your heels as high as you can. Keep your toes on the board. Then lower your heels to the starting position, and repeat the exercise.

Calf raises from a standing position are more difficult. Stand erect with a barbell resting across your upper back and shoulders, as if you were about to do a half squat (see above). Your toes should be resting on the board, so the balls of your feet are elevated.

Keeping your back straight and without bending your legs, rise as high as you can on your toes.

Then lower yourself until your heels touch the floor again.

Other exercises for strengthening the legs require what is called an "iron boot." This takes the form of a metal plate in the shape of the sole of the shoe which attaches to your athletic shoe or sneaker. The bar of a dumbbell attaches to the iron boot, enabling you to perform a variety of leg exercises. For example, you can wear an iron boot and a dumbbell on your right foot. Then, standing on your left foot on a bench or a chair, you bend your right leg up behind your body. This exercise is useful in developing the thigh muscles.

Or, from a seated position, you can do leg extensions with the weighted foot that strengthen the quadriceps muscle of that leg. After a series of repetitions with one leg, you switch the boot to the other foot.

If you want to try some of these drills, but don't care to buy an iron boot, try taping plates to an old pair of shoes. Don the right shoe and exercise the right leg. Then exercise with the left shoe. It's not quite as efficient as if you were wearing an iron boot, but it gets the job done.

Calf raises from a standing position are no cinch. Begin with the heels touching the floor, then rise on your toes as high as you can.

When doing sit-ups, use a barbell to anchor your feet. Clamp your hands behind your head.

TRIMMING THE WAIST

To keep your midsection trim and firm, there are four basic exercises you can do. They strengthen the muscles of the belly and the sides, just above the hips.

One of these exercises is well known to you: it's the sit-up. Sit-ups develop the muscles at the front of the upper abdomen, or belly. Leg raises are recommended for the lower abdominal muscles. Many weight lifters, incidentally, refer to the upper and lower abdominal muscles as "abs."

SIT-UP—To do a sit-up, lie on your back on the floor, bending your knees slightly. (Bending the knees takes the strain off your lower back.) Anchor your feet beneath the bar of a heavily weighted barbell. Clasp your hands behind your head.

Take a deep breath and sit up, exhaling as you rise. Touch your elbows to your knees. Inhale as you return to the starting position. Try doing this as many as 10 or 20 times

After you've been doing conventional sit-ups for

eight to ten weeks, try advanced sit-ups, ones involving weights. Begin with a dumbbell or a barbell plate weighing 2½ or five pounds. Hold the dumbbell behind your head as you do the exercise. Try to do as many as ten sit-ups of this type. When this exercise becomes easy, add 2½ pounds.

LEG RAISE—It's possible to do this exercise while lying on the floor but it's more effective if you lie on an exercise bench. Grasp the sides of the bench near your hips. Extend your legs. Allowing your knees to bend slightly, raise your legs until they reach an angle of 45 degrees. Then lower them until they are parallel to the floor again, pause, and repeat the exercise.

Inhale as you raise your legs, making an extra effort to draw in your belly. Exhale as you lower them.

The leg raise is another good exercise for developing the abdominal muscles.

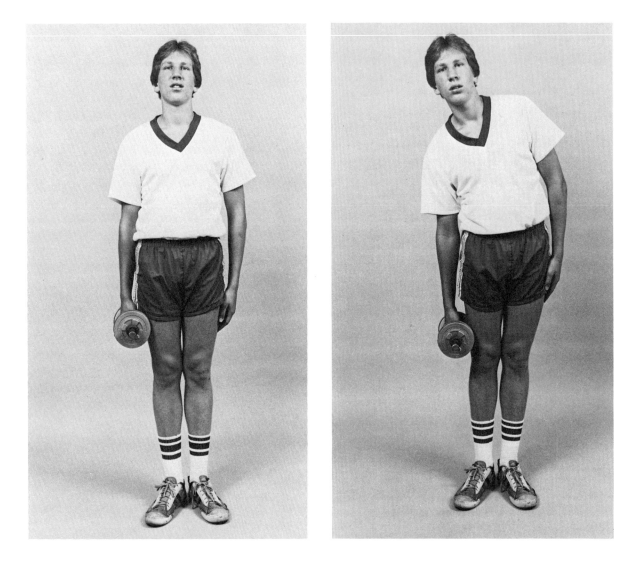

Try doing at least ten leg raises, increasing the number by one a week as your muscles get stronger. With experienced athletes, three sets of 20 leg raises and a single set of 50 are not uncommon.

SIDE BEND—This exercise strengthens both the internal and external oblique muscles, the muscles of the side just above the waist.

Holding a lightweight dumbbell in your right hand, and tucking your left hand behind your back, bend sideways to the right as far as you can go. Pause, straighten up, then bend to the left side, pause, and straighten. Then switch the dumbbell to your left hand, place your right hand behind your back, and repeat the drill. Do as many as ten repetitions on each side.

SIDE TWIST—This exercise involves the use of the barbell bar with no weights attached. Hold the bar across the back of your shoulders, gripping it at each end. Stand erect and spread your feet wide apart. Bending at the waist, twist to the right as far as you can go, or until the bar forms right angles with the floor. Pause, return to the starting position, and then twist in the other direction. Try doing a total of from 10 to 20 repetitions, five to ten in each direction. This exercise not only serves to trim the midsection, it also conditions the muscles of your sides.

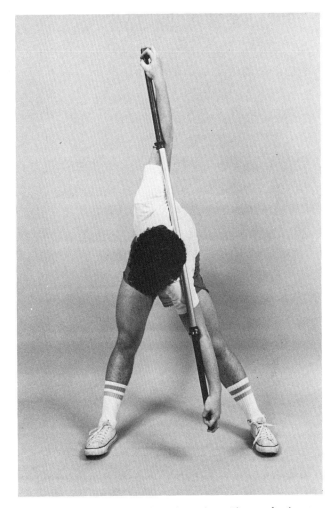

Opposite: Side bends strengthen the muscles of the sides just above the waist.

Use the barbell bar to do side twists. First twist in one direction, then the other, going as far as you can go.

A PROGRAM OF YOUR OWN

Once you've become skilled and experienced in performing the exercises described in this book, you can put together your own weight-training program. The idea is to choose a goal, then select the exercises that will help you achieve it.

At the beginning, you should be concerned about developing as much all-around strength as possible. Thus, select six or seven exercises which will, in total, contribute to body fitness as a whole. Your program might include:

> Barbell Curl (arms)
> Overhead Press (shoulders)
> Push-up (chest)
> Flyaway (chest)
> Bent-over Rowing (back)
> Half Squat (legs and thighs)
> Sit-up (waist)

When you feel you've made significant improvement in your overall strength, try setting other goals for yourself. Let's say you want to put more emphasis on the development of your arms and chest. Then you might add a triceps extension (for the arms) and a straight-arm pullover (for the chest) in place of two of the other exercises that make up your program.

Or you may want to plan an exercise program that develops the muscles that are important for certain sports. Think about how you use your body

in these sports. Then you'll come to an appreciation of how weight training can help you.

If you're a football lineman, for example, you'll want to do exercises that concentrate on leg and shoulder development—half squats and calf raises for the legs, and overhead presses and lateral raises for the shoulders.

To excel in tennis, you have to be able to start fast and make abrupt stops. Lunges and side twists will help you in this regard.

A powerful swing comes from strong legs, arms, and shoulders, plus a twisting motion of the upper body. For the legs, do the front squat. For the torso, do twists. The various barbell and dumbbell curls, raises, and presses are important.

It's a good idea to get your coach's advice when developing such a program. The exercises you choose have to be tailored very specifically for the demands the sport makes upon you. If you're a sprinter on your school's track team, you'll be asked to do different exercises than those given a middle distance or cross-country specialist. Choosing the wrong exercise actually can be harmful to your development.

Once you've embarked on a weight-training program, stick with it for at least four to six weeks. Beginners sometimes make the mistake of changing their routines when they fail to see immediate results. You have to be persistent. Your program *can* produce surprising results. But don't expect them to occur overnight.

COMPETITIVE WEIGHT LIFTING

Weight lifting is more than merely a means of improving your strength and health. It is also a competitive sport.

Competitive weight lifting first became popular in Central Europe during the early 1800s. It spread from there to the Scandinavian countries, and Egypt, Turkey, and Japan. The sport was introduced to the United States about one hundred years ago.

Competitive weight lifting has been an Olympic event since 1896. By 1920, the year in which the International Weight Lifting Federation was founded, organized weight lifting had reached about every part of the world.

There are two basic lifts in competitive weight lifting: the snatch and the clean and jerk. In the snatch, the lifter picks up the weighted barbell with both hands and raises it in one continuous motion to a position directly overhead with the arms extended. Once the lifter is motionless "in all parts of his body," to quote the rulebook, the referee gives him the "Down" signal.

In the clean and jerk, the lifter raises the weight to shoulder level, pauses briefly, and then thrusts the weight overhead, the arms extended. Once the weight has been jerked and is held motionless, the referee signals it can be put down.

Scores of the two lifts are added together to determine the winner. Individuals compete in various

Barbells of the type used by competitive lifters

weight divisions, ranging from flyweight and bantamweight to super heavyweight.

Competitive weight lifting in the United States is governed by the United States Weightlifting Federation. That organization offers a Junior Olympic Program for young lifters. The program is part of the AAU (Amateur Athletic Union) Junior Olympics Program.

Approximately three million young athletes, ages

six to eighteen, take part in the program each year. Competition is offered in a total of eighteen different sports.

Weight-lifting competition involves the two Olympic lifts, the snatch and the clean and jerk. You compete in your own age group. There are four age-group divisions:

JUNIOR DIVISION
(Age 12 and 13)

82½ lbs. (37.5 kg.)
93½ lbs. (42.5 kg.)
104½ lbs. (47.5 kg.)
114½ lbs. (52 kg.)
123½ lbs. (56 kg.)
132¼ lbs. (60 kg.)
148¾ lbs. (67.5 kg.)
165¼ lbs. (75 kg.)
Over 165¼ lbs. (75 kg.)

JR. INTERMEDIATE DIVISION
(Age 14 and 15)

104½ lbs. (47.5 kg.)
114½ lbs. (52 kg.)
123½ lbs. (56 kg.)
132¼ lbs. (60 kg.)
148¾ lbs. (67.5 kg.)
165¼ lbs. (75 kg.)
181¾ lbs. (82.5 kg.)
198¼ lbs. (90 kg.)
Over 198¼ lbs. (90 kg.)

INTERMEDIATE DIVISION
(Age 16 and 17)

114½ lbs. (50 kg.)
123½ lbs. (56 kg.)
132¼ lbs. (60 kg.)
148¾ lbs. (67.5 kg.)
165¼ lbs. (75 kg.)
181¾ lbs. (82.5 kg.)
198¼ lbs. (90 kg.)
Over 198¼ lbs. (90 kg.)

SENIOR DIVISION
(Age 18 and 19)

114½ lbs. (52 kg.)
123½ lbs. (56 kg.)
132¼ lbs. (60 kg.)
148¾ lbs. (67.5 kg.)
165¼ lbs. (75 kg.)
181¾ lbs. (82.5 kg.)
198¼ lbs. (90 kg.)
242½ lbs. (110 kg.)
Over 242½ lbs. (110 kg.)

Competition begins on a local level. Lifters who excel on the local level advance to the association championships, conducted among the AAU's fifty-eight geographical sectors. The association champions go on to the regional championships. There are fifteen AAU regions. Regional champions advance to the national championships.

You can find out more about the program by requesting information from the United States Weight-lifting Federation (1750 East Boulder Street, Colorado Springs, CO 80909) or a local office of the AAU.

A new development in weight lifting took place in 1972, when the International Powerlifting Federation was formed. In powerlifting, individuals, again grouped in weight divisions, compete in these events: the bench press, squat, and dead lift. (These terms are defined earlier in this book and in the glossary.) Almost every major college in the United States now holds powerlifting contests.

GLOSSARY

AB—Short for abdominal muscles.

ABDOMEN—The belly.

ABDOMINAL—Referring to the abdomen, or belly.

AUTONOMIC NERVOUS SYSTEM—The part of the nervous system made up of the nerves and nerve tissue common to the blood vessels, heart, glands, and intestines.

BAR—Short for barbell.

BARBELL—A steel bar, usually five to six feet in length, that is fitted with plates at each end. The plates are held in place by adjustable metal collars.

BENCH PRESS—An exercise in which one lies on his back on a bench; then, using the arms, shoulders, and chest, thrusts the barbell up from the chest.

BICEPS—The muscle at the front of the upper arm.

CALF—The fleshy part of the leg below the back of the knee.

CARDIAC MUSCLE—The muscle of the heart.

CARDIOVASCULAR SYSTEM—The bodily system that includes the heart and blood vessels.

CENTRAL NERVOUS SYSTEM—The part of the nervous system made up of the brain and spinal cord.

CLEAN AND JERK—A lift in which the lifter raises the barbell from the floor to shoulder level, pauses, then thrusts the weight overhead.

COLLAR—A circular fitting with a screw or other tightening device that fits over the end of a barbell or dumbbell to hold a plate in place. Two collars are used for each plate.

CURL—An exercise in which dumbbells, or a barbell, are held at thigh level, then raised to chest or shoulder level without any movement of the shoulders or upper arm.

DEAD LIFT—An exercise in which one squats and grasps a barbell, then raises to stand erect, holding the barbell with straight arms across the upper thighs.

DELTOID—The large triangular muscle that caps the shoulder.

DUMBBELL—A short bar fitted with plates of equal size and weight at each end, and designed to be used with one hand.

FLY—See Flyaway.

FLYAWAY—An exercise performed with dumbbells while lying on the back, the arms straight out to the sides. The weights are raised and lowered repeatedly, a motion that resembles a bird's wings in flight. Also called the fly.

HAMSTRING—The muscles at the back of the thighbone and knee; also the tendons at the back, or hollow, of the knee.

HERNIA—A split or tear in the muscle wall of an organ which allows the organ to protrude.

INVOLUNTARY MUSCLE—One of the muscles that line the internal organs, and which functions without one's conscious direction.

IRON BOOT—A metal plate in the shape of the sole of a shoe which can be attached to the foot, and to which the bar of a dumbbell can be fixed, so that weight may be attached to the foot for leg exercises.

LATISSIMUS DORSI—A broad flat muscle on each side of the back, running from under the arms to the waist.

LATS—Short for latissimus dorsi muscle.

LIGAMENT—A band of tissue that connects one bone to another.

OBLIQUE MUSCLES—The muscles of the sides, just above the waist.

OVERHAND GRIP—A method of grasping the bar in which the knuckles are placed above the bar.

PECTORAL MUSCLES—Fairly large muscles that cover the entire chest.

PECS—Short for pectoral muscles.

PLATE—A metal disk, sometimes plastic-covered, that has a specific weight. Plates of equal size and weight are fitted to each end of a barbell or dumbbell in weight-training exercises.

PRESS—A lift in which a dumbbell or barbell is pushed up from shoulder level to a position straight overhead using the strength of the arms, shoulders, and back, and without movement of the feet or legs.

QUADRICEPS—The large muscle at the front of the thigh.

REP—See Repetition.

REPETITION—A single performance of an exercise from the starting position, through the full range of the exercise, and back to the starting position. Also called a rep.

SET—A specific number of repetitions.

SKELETAL MUSCLE—Any of the muscles that control physical movement.

SLEEVE—The tubular length of metal that fits over the bar of a barbell to aid in gripping.

SNATCH—A lift in which the lifter raises the barbell from the floor and raises it in one continuous motion to a position overhead.

SPOTTER—Someone, usually a coach or other weight lifter, who assists the exerciser by holding him or helping him to adjust the weight.

SPRAIN—An injury involving a ligament that results when one overstrains or wrenches an ankle, wrist, or other part of the body at a joint.

SQUAT—A lift in which one squats all the way down, then rises again to a standing position while holding the barbell behind his head, resting it on the back of the shoulders.

STRAIN—An injury that occurs through the overextension of a muscle or tendon.

TENDON—A cord of tough, white, fibrous tissue at the end of a muscle, and which connects the muscle to a bone.

TRAPEZIUS—The broad, flat muscle on each side of the upper and back part of the shoulders and neck.

TRICEPS—The muscle at the back of the upper arm, used in straightening the arm.

UNDERHAND GRIP—A method of grasping the bar in which the knuckles are placed beneath the bar.